LeBRON JAMES

REAL BiOS

By Marie Morreale

Children's Press®
An Imprint of Scholastic Inc.
New York   Toronto   London   Auckland   Sydney
Mexico City   New Delhi   Hong Kong
Danbury, Connecticut

Photographs ©: AP Images: 23 top, 24 bottom (Amy Sancetta), 25 (Bill Haber), 27 (Charles Dharapak), 28 (Charles Krupa), 42 top (Charles Sykes), 23 bottom (Dusan Vranic), 32 (Evan Vucci), 42 center, 13 bottom right, 24 top (J.Pat Carter), 39 right (Jae C. Hong), 38 bottom (John Swart), 20 top (LM Otero), 26, 29, 30 (Lynne Sladky), back cover (Matt Slocum), 15 top right (Nickelodeon), 18 (Rich Pedroncelli), 6, 7 (Rich Schultz), 15 top left (Sharon Ellman), 13 top right, 41 top (Steve C. Wilson), 36 (Stuart Ramson), 8, 22 (Tony Dejak), 38 top (Wilfredo Lee); Dreamstime: 15 center left (Hupeng), 43 (Ingvar Bjork), 15 bottom left (Scruggelgreen); Getty Images/ Noam Galai: 42 center; iStockphoto/Arsela: 37; The LeBron James Family Foundation: 9; Newscom: 1, 14 (Albert Pena/ Cal Sport Media), 34 (Ed Suba Jr./KRT), 2, 3 (Gary Coronado/ Zuma Press), 40 (infusmi-11/13/INFphoto.com), 10 (Lucy Nicholson/AFP), 33 (Meng Yongmin/Chine Nouvel/Sipa), 13 bottom left (Phil Masturzo/Akron Beacon Journal/MCT), 17 (Phil Masturzo/KRT); Redux/Gian Marco Castelberg/13 Photo/R: cover; Reuters: 41 bottom (Aaron Josefczyk), 35 (Joe Skipper), 44 (Mark J. Rebilas-USA Today Sports), 4, 5 (Robert Mayer-USA Today Sports); Rex USA : 20 bottom, 21 (c.Lions Gate/Everett), 16 (Everett); Shutterstock, Inc.: 13 top left (bestv), 15 bottom right (JStone), 13 top left (Lightspring), 39 left (Valentina Razumova); Zuma Press/Pedro Portal/MCT: 12.

Library of Congress Cataloging-in-Publication Data
Morreale, Marie.
  LeBron James / by Marie Morreale.
    pages cm. — (Real bios)
  Includes bibliographical references and index.
  ISBN 978-0-531-21198-4 (lib. bdg. : alk. paper) —
ISBN 978-0-531-21273-8 (pbk. : alk. paper)
  1. James, LeBron—Juvenile literature. 2. Basketball players—
United States—Biography—Juvenile literature. 3. African
American basketball players—Biography—Juvenile literature.
I. Title.
  GV884.J36M68 2014
  796.323092—dc23[B]   2014004443

Printed in the United States of America 113
SCHOLASTIC, CHILDREN'S PRESS, and associated logos are trademarks and/or registered trademarks of Scholastic Inc.

1 2 3 4 5 6 7 8 9 10 R 24 23 22 21 20 19 18 17 16 15

LeBron James thanks Miami Heat fans at the opening night of the 2013-2014 season!

MEET LEBRON JAMES!

HE WEARS HIS "KING" CROWN WELL!

LeBron James—King James to his fans—is one of the world's biggest sports superstars. He played football and basketball in high school, and went on to a headline-making career in the NBA. He has won back-to-back championship rings with his team, the Miami Heat. In this Real Bio, you'll find out how the only child of a single mom lived a rags-to-riches story. You'll see how hard work and sacrifice took him from the streets of Akron, Ohio, to the top of his game. And you'll meet the people who helped make it all possible. Just for fun, you'll become a whiz kid about King James's faves, fun facts, and info. You'll see photos of LeBron on the court, with family, friends, and teammates . . . and even with First Lady Michelle and President Barack Obama. That's pretty cool company to keep!

Okay, wait for the tip-off . . . then read!

CONTENTS

Meet LeBron James! 3

CHAPTER ONE
He Got Game.............. 6

CHAPTER TWO
NBA Dreams............. 18

CHAPTER THREE
Q&A........................ 30

CHAPTER FOUR
Bits & Pieces.............. 36

CHAPTER FIVE
What's Next?.............. 44

Resources 46
Glossary 46
Index....................... 47
Acknowledgments........ 48
About the Author......... 48

And it's a dunk for King James!

"I'M NOT JUST SAYING, 'LET'S WORK HARD, LET'S DO THIS, LET'S SACRIFICE. I'M DOING THOSE THINGS THAT I'M PREACHING. . . . IT'S JUST WHO I AM."

LEBRON JAMES'S

HOOPS JOURNEY

HOW HE WENT FROM "BRON BRON" TO THE "CHOSEN 1"

Future NBA Hall of Fame superstar LeBron James was born on December 30, 1984, in Akron, Ohio. His mom, Gloria James, was only 16 years old, and his father was no longer in the picture. There definitely would be a lot of obstacles ahead for them. But the James family—his mom, his grandmother, Freda, and his uncles Terry and Curt—surrounded little LeBron with love. After LeBron was born, Gloria went back to school and also worked. Though there wasn't a lot of money, they got by.

When LeBron was only two years old, his grandmother suddenly passed away. The loss was devastating to the James family. They missed the love, guidance, and security that Freda had given them. Less than a year later, they realized they couldn't afford the upkeep on the family

As St. Vincent-St. Mary High School's star player, LeBron goes for a layup!

On the Court
In high school, LeBron was nicknamed the Chosen 1.

LeBron's mom, Gloria, congratulates him after a St. Vincent-St. Mary's championship.

house, and they had to move out. LeBron was five years old. He and his mom found shelter with friends and family. But they never had a permanent address.

By the time LeBron was eight years old, he and Gloria had moved at least 12 times. This meant LeBron never stayed at one school for very long. He didn't have many friends, and he missed a lot of school.

Little did LeBron and Gloria know that an accidental meeting would end up changing their lives forever. They had been staying at a friend's housing project apartment in downtown Akron. One day, Gloria was outside watching LeBron and some of his friends playing. A local recreational league football coach named Bruce Kelker stopped by to see if he could find some kids to try out for his team, the East Dragons. He challenged the boys to compete in a 100-yard footrace and announced that the winner would be the team's **running back**. LeBron easily won. Kelker was so impressed with his new **protégé** that he offered to pay for LeBron's equipment and give him rides to practice and games.

Because Gloria and LeBron moved so much, there were times that Kelker didn't know where to pick LeBron up. He came up with a solution. Gloria and LeBron would move into his house with him and his wife. At last, Team James had some stability. When it came time for Gloria and LeBron to move again, another one of the coaches, Frank Walker, invited the youngster to live with him and his family. LeBron

A ten-year-old LeBron (standing next to the coach) poses with his first basketball team and Coach Frank Walker.

shared a bedroom with Frank's son, Frankie Jr., who was already a good friend from the East Dragons. Gloria decided to stay with a friend and look for a steady job so she could earn enough money to set up a real home for her and LeBron. But she visited LeBron at the Walker house every weekend. She also attended every East Dragons game to cheer on her "Bron Bron."

While living with the Walkers, LeBron had to get up at 6:30 every morning, go to school, do household chores, and finish his homework before he could go outside and play—just like the Walker kids. When football season was over, LeBron wanted to try his hand at basketball. Coach

LeBron's number one cheerleader, mom Gloria, watches him play at a St. Vincent-St. Mary's game.

Walker taught him some moves and saw that LeBron had natural skills on the court. LeBron signed up to play on a basketball team for nine-year-olds. LeBron learned principles that would be important for the rest of his life— dedication, time management, hard work, and setting goals. The best sign of his new attitude was that he was going to school every day and getting good grades!

LeBron was finally on the right track. Soon, he and Gloria got their own apartment in Akron's Elizabeth Park housing projects. LeBron, who was now in the fifth grade, was getting more and more attention on the basketball court. He regularly played at the Summit Lake Community Center. That was where basketball coach Dru Joyce first saw him. Impressed with LeBron's natural abilities, Coach Dru asked Gloria if she would let her son join his team, the Shooting Stars. When she said yes, Coach Dru had the beginnings of his own Dream Team.

Speedy Learner
"I had never coached a kid who picked things up and excelled in them as quickly as LeBron."— Frank Walker Sr., LeBron's first coach

Coach Dru's son, Dru Joyce III, was an early addition to the team. He had been shooting hoops since almost before he started to walk! The next member of the team was Sian Cotton, the son of a successful Akron high school basketball coach, Lee Cotton. LeBron, Little Dru, and Sian quickly became the central unit of the Shooting Stars. The team was invited to participate in the national Amateur Athletic Union (AAU) tournament in Cocoa Beach, Florida. All participants were 11 years old or younger. The Shooting Stars came in ninth out of 64 teams! Coach Dru told the boys that he knew it was just the beginning of something special.

Fifth grade . . . sixth grade . . . seventh grade . . . LeBron played on the Shooting Stars and the Summit Lake Hornets basketball team and kept his grades up.

FACT FILE

THE BASICS

Basketball Boy

"I think [I] knew I loved basketball towards the end of seventh or eighth grade. . . . I just kept working at it."
—LeBron James

FULL NAME LeBron Raymone James

NICKNAMES Bron Bron, Chosen 1, King James, LBJ

BIRTHDAY December 30, 1984

ASTROLOGICAL SIGN Capricorn

BIRTHPLACE Akron, Ohio

CURRENT HOMES Coconut Grove, Florida, and Akron, Ohio

PARENTS Mother, Gloria James; father, Anthony McClelland

WIFE Savannah Brinson James

CHILDREN Sons, LeBron James Jr. (born October 6, 2004) and Bryce Maximus James (born June 14, 2007)

HEIGHT 6'8"

PEE WEE FOOTBALL TEAM The South Rangers—he played tailback

HIGH SCHOOL St. Vincent-St. Mary

HIGH SCHOOL SPORTS Basketball and football

BASKETBALL HONOR Named "Mr. Basketball" in Ohio during his sophomore year of high school

HIGH SCHOOL JERSEY NUMBER 23, in honor of basketball icon Michael Jordan

SPECIAL CHARITIES Boys & Girls Clubs of America, Children's Defense Fund, ONEXONE, LeBron James Family Foundation

NBA POSITIONS Small forward, power forward, shooting guard

NBA PALS Dwyane Wade and Chris Bosh

TWITTER @KingJames

It was on the Hornets that LeBron met Willie McGee. Willie soon became part of the inner circle with LeBron, Little Dru, and Sian. Once the guys reached eighth grade, they decided to go to St. Vincent-St. Mary, also known as St. V. St. V's basketball team was not one of the best around, but LeBron and his friends thought they could work together to take St. V to the top. During LeBron's freshman year, the Akron press took notice of him and his friends, nicknaming them the Fab Four.

St. V won the Ohio state championship in 2000. LeBron, Willie, Little Dru, and Sian were

FACT FILE

FAVORITES

Basketball Alternative

"I would probably be playing football. I really loved playing it in high school."

VIDEO GAME
The Madden NFL series

FOOTBALL TEAM
Dallas Cowboys

BASEBALL TEAM
New York Yankees

NFL QUARTERBACK Tom Brady of the
New England Patriots

CAR
Maybach

ACTRESS Halle Berry

DIGITAL ACCESSORIES Beats by Dr. Dre
headphones, his smartphone

PREGAME MEAL Fish,
broccoli, rice

CEREAL Fruity Pebbles

FOOD Fried chicken

DESSERT German chocolate cake

PIECE OF JEWELRY
His lion head chain

BOOK SERIES AS A KID
Goosebumps
by R. L. Stine

CARTOON
SpongeBob
SquarePants—
"I watch cartoons
even when my kids
are in school!"

SUBJECTS IN SCHOOL
Math and earth science

CARTOON CHARACTER Batman

TV SERIES The Simpsons

SPORTS MOVIES Ali, Hoop Dreams,
The Program, Blue Chips, Hoosiers

MUSIC Rap

RAP ARTIST
Jay-Z—"I listen to Jay-Z
before every game.
Every album he's
got. Every song."

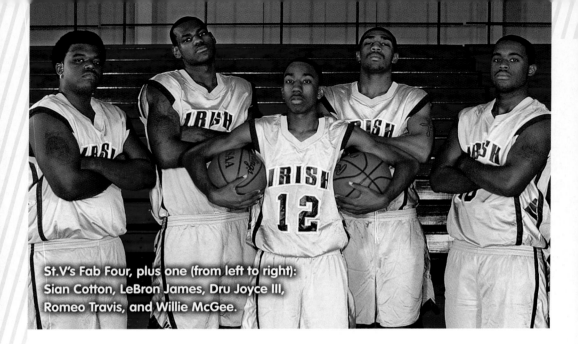

St.V's Fab Four, plus one (from left to right):
Sian Cotton, LeBron James, Dru Joyce III,
Romeo Travis, and Willie McGee.

only freshmen! But their sophomore year held a change. Their coach wanted his team to be more than just the Fab Four plus a rotating team member. They needed a full-time fifth man to fill out the starting lineup. When Romeo Travis transferred to St. V that year, he seemed to be the final ingredient to the recipe. It baked—they won the Ohio state championship again in 2001. Back-to-back championships!

Before LeBron's junior season, the team's coach left to coach a college team. He was replaced by Coach Dru. There was going to be a lot of pressure on Coach Dru and the team to win the championship again. They were right to worry. That year, the team failed to win the state championship. LeBron admits they had gotten too full of themselves—"Too much media attention, too little attention to basketball," he wrote of the season in his book *Shooting Stars*.

Senior year was a turning point for the St. V basketball team. They proved themselves by winning not only the Ohio state championship, but the national championship as well. They were the number one team in the entire country!

"I couldn't help but think how all of this had started in the fifth grade, that little kernel we never gave up on," LeBron wrote in *Shooting Stars*. "We had accomplished our goal, and as members of the Fab Five we had done it in the last game of basketball we would ever play together."

They all went in different directions. But Willie, Romeo, Sian, and Little Dru kept cheering for LeBron as he made his way to the NBA.

June 7, 2003—High school graduation day for LeBron and "Irish" teammate and bestie, Dru Joyce III.

Being a Champ

"I have short goals—to get better every day, to help my teammates every day—but my only ultimate goal is to win an NBA championship."

Cleveland Cavaliers rookie LeBron goes for a layup during his first NBA game.

KING JAMES RULES

THE UPS AND DOWNS OF HIS NBA CAREER

LeBron played his very first NBA game on October 29, 2003, when the Cleveland Cavaliers met the Sacramento Kings. He racked up 25 points, nine assists, and four steals to lead the Cavs to victory. That season, LeBron's spark helped the Cavs win 18 more games than they had the year before.

The Cavs continued to improve during the 2004–05 season, and LeBron broke more and more records. He was picked as a **starter** for the Eastern Conference in the NBA All-Star Game. In the 2005–06 season, the Cavs made it to the **playoffs** for the first time in six years, though they lost to the Detroit Pistons before reaching the finals.

LeBron was all geared up for the 2006–07 season. That year, the Cavaliers advanced to the NBA Finals. Unfortunately, the San Antonio Spurs beat them. More determined than ever, LeBron entered the next season ready to go all the way. He led the entire NBA in scoring

He's flying! LeBron is named MVP of the 2006 NBA All-Star Game.

for the year. Even with LeBron's amazing stats, the Cavs lost to the Boston Celtics in the playoffs before reaching the finals.

The NBA championship ring seemed just out of reach. Every season since LeBron joined the team, the Cavaliers had gotten better and better. They seemed close to reaching the ultimate goal. In the 2008–09 season, the Cavs made it to the Eastern Conference Finals, just out of reach of the NBA Finals. Unfortunately, they were defeated by the Orlando Magic.

LeBron's Timeline

LeBron Brings the House Down

DECEMBER 30, 1984
LeBron Raymone James is born.

MARCH 25, 2000
As a freshman at the St. Vincent-St. Mary High School, he leads the basketball team to the state championship.

LeBron and his St. Vincent-St. Mary teammates

The 2009–10 season was going to be a very important one for LeBron. At the end of the season, he would become a free agent, which meant that he could possibly leave the Cavs to play for a different team. But that wasn't on his mind when the season started. The Cavaliers had the best record in the NBA. They aimed toward the championship once again, but they were defeated in the play-offs by the Boston Celtics.

The summer of 2010 was a time for LeBron to make some important decisions. There was widespread speculation about whether he would join a new team. LeBron made his changes slowly. First, he announced that he was changing his jersey number from 23 to 6, in honor of his son LeBron Jr., who had been

Achieving Your Goals

"If I get to a spot in a workout and want to make 8 out of 10, if I don't make 8 of 10, then I run. I push myself to the point of exhaustion until I make that goal."

FEBRUARY 18, 2002
He is on the cover of *Sports Illustrated*, with the headline "The Chosen One."

MARCH 17, 2003
LeBron becomes the first player ever to be named Ohio's "Mr. Basketball" three times.

born on October 6. Next he would reveal whether or not that number 6 would be on a different team's jersey.

LeBron chose to make his decision known in an hour-long TV show called *The Decision*. Sports fans around the country watched in anticipation, waiting for LeBron to make the announcement. Finally, near the end of the show, he revealed that he was joining the Miami Heat.

The Cavaliers and their fans felt that LeBron had let them down. Sportswriters argued that LeBron's choice to announce his decision on a TV show had been tacky. And when it was reported that one of the reasons LeBron had signed with the Heat was because he felt they had the best chance to win the 2010–11 NBA championship, he was called selfish. LeBron was a bit surprised at the angry reaction and the headlines that screamed, "LeBron James—The Most

The Move
"I'm the same person. I just want to win."

MARCH 22, 2003
He leads St. Vincent-St. Mary High School to the AAU National Championship.

JUNE 26, 2003
He is chosen by the Cleveland Cavaliers as the number one pick in the NBA draft.

OCTOBER 29, 2003
LeBron makes his NBA debut.

JAMES
23

Hated Player in Basketball." Later on, he told *USA Today*, "During my first seven years in the NBA I was always the liked one. To be on the other side, they call it the dark side, or the villain, whatever they call it. . . . It was definitely challenging for [me]. It was a situation I had never been in before. I took a long time to adjust to it. It didn't feel good. I was still living in Ohio and you could feel it. You don't even have to hear it. You can feel it. . . .

Cleveland Cav fans were disappointed when LeBron announced his move to the Miami Heat. The *Cleveland Plain Dealer*'s July 9, 2010, front page showed it.

APRIL 20, 2004
LeBron becomes the youngest player ever to be named NBA Rookie of the Year.

AUGUST 28, 2004
LeBron and Team USA win the bronze medal at the Summer Olympic

Games in Athens, Greece.

JUNE 14, 2007
LeBron leads the Cavs to the NBA Finals, but they lose to the San Antonio Spurs in a four-game sweep.

AUGUST 24, 2008
LeBron and Team USA win an Olympic gold medal in Beijing, China.

If I could look back on it, I would probably change a lot of it. The fact of having a whole TV special, and people getting the opportunity to watch me make a decision on where I wanted to play, I probably would change that. Because I can now look and see if the shoe was on the other foot and I was a fan, and I was very passionate about one player, and he decided to leave, I would be upset too about the way he handled it."

MAY 4, 2009
LeBron wins his first NBA MVP title.

JULY 8, 2010
LeBron announces he has signed with the Miami Heat on ESPN in *The Decision.*

JUNE 2011
LeBron and the Heat play in the NBA Finals, but lose to the Dallas Mavericks.

JUNE 2012
The Miami Heat win the NBA Finals against the Oklahoma City Thunder.

Cavs fans were upset with LeBron, but Heat supporters were chanting his name as soon as he hit the court in Miami. During the 2010–11 season, LeBron was asked to play several different roles on the team. He realized he had to adjust his game to perform his new duties. After playing with the same team for six years, he had to work on fitting in with the Heat's style of play. He had to learn to play alongside his new teammates, including fellow superstars Dwyane Wade and Chris Bosh.

It didn't help that LeBron was greeted with boos and jeers from his former fans the first time he returned to Cleveland to play

Not just a scorer, LeBron defends the hoop, too—this time against Trevor Ariza of the Hornets.

AUGUST 12, 2012
LeBron and Team USA win their second gold medal at the Summer Olympic Games in London, England.

JUNE 2013
The Miami Heat defeat the San Antonio Spurs

in the NBA Finals to win their second straight championship title.

JANUARY 14, 2014
LeBron and the Heat visit the White House and are congratulated on the NBA championship by

President Obama.

JUNE 15, 2014
The Heat lose the NBA Finals to the Spurs.

JULY 11, 2014
LeBron announces his return to the Cleveland Cavaliers.

against the Cavs. But LeBron and the Heat soon got into sync. They marched all the way to the NBA Finals, where they faced off against the Dallas Mavericks. Everyone was watching to see if LeBron James could win his first NBA championship ring. He didn't. The Heat lost to the Mavericks, and LeBron's stats during the finals were nowhere near his best.

LeBron knew he had to shake something up. He didn't have time to feel sorry for himself. He just wanted to get better. So, that summer, before the Heat started their preseason workouts, LeBron went to legendary NBA superstar Hakeem Olajuwon for guidance. Olajuwon had led the Houston Rockets to back-to-back NBA championships in the 1990s. He was inducted into the Basketball Hall of Fame in 2008 and is considered one of the greatest **centers** in basketball history.

No smile on LeBron's face. This time the Heat lost to the Mavericks.

At the White House, President Obama honors LeBron and the Heat for their 2012 NBA championship.

White House Visit "It's an honor as a team to get to be able to go to the White House and be with the president."

When asked by a reporter from Grantland.com why he visited Olajuwon, LeBron said, "I wanted to get better. I wanted to improve and I sought out someone who I thought was one of the greatest . . . to ever play this game. I was grateful and happy that he welcomed me with open arms. . . . He taught me a lot about . . . being able to gain an advantage on your opponent. I used that the rest of the off-season, when I went back to my hometown. Every day in the gym I worked on one thing or I worked on two things and tried to improve every day."

Going for the Gold

- LeBron played for Team USA at the 2004 Summer Olympic Games in Athens, Greece. The team came home with a bronze medal.

- LeBron returned to Team USA for the 2008 Summer Olympic Games in Beijing, China. This time, they came home with a gold medal.

- Once again, LeBron joined Team USA for the 2012 Summer Olympic Games in London, England. The team won another gold medal. Back-to-back Olympic gold!

When LeBron returned after the summer break, Heat coach Erik Spoelstra was amazed. "He was a totally different player," Spoelstra told Grantland.com. "It was as if he downloaded a program with all of Olajuwon's . . . moves. I don't know if I've seen a player improve that much in a specific area in one off-season."

Everything clicked during the 2011–12 season. LeBron was named NBA MVP, and the Heat went on to defeat the Oklahoma City Thunder in the NBA Finals. LeBron finally had an NBA championship ring!

The 2012–13 season was very important to LeBron and his teammates. They wanted to prove they weren't just one-time winners. That season, the Heat racked up the best record in the league and LeBron was named the NBA MVP for the fourth time. Best of all, the Heat beat the San Antonio Spurs in the finals for their second straight NBA championship. Ring number two!

Somehow LeBron also found time for some off-court hustle. At a return White House Miami Heat visit, LeBron shot a public service announcement (PSA) for the U.S. health care law. Reports also came out that LeBron is in discussion to coproduce a TV sitcom!

The 2013–14 season brought the Heat to right where they had left off the year before: facing off against the San Antonio Spurs in the NBA Finals. Despite a strong performance from LeBron and the Heat, the Spurs won this time. Perhaps that helped LeBron decide to return home to the Cleveland Cavaliers for the 2014–15 season!

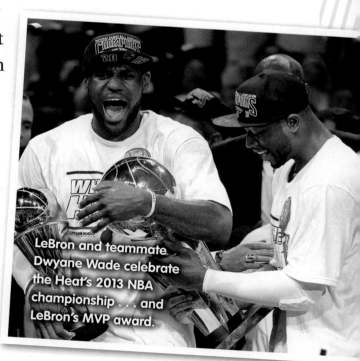

LeBron and teammate Dwyane Wade celebrate the Heat's 2013 NBA championship . . . and LeBron's MVP award.

LeBron, Dwyane Wade,
and Chris Bosh at a
Heat press conference.

WHAT LEBRON SAYS!

KING JAMES TALKS BASKETBALL, VEGETABLES, PERSONAL IDOLS, AND MORE!

Wherever LeBron James is, everyone wants to ask questions—"Are you going to win the championship this year?". . . "Are you going to stay with the Miami Heat?". . . "What's your favorite food?"

That's right, queries come from left and right on every subject known to man. One of the cool things about LeBron is that he tries to answer questions whenever he can—especially if they come from young fans. He is willing to share his story in hopes that it might help others. It has!

On winning his second NBA championship with the Miami Heat . . . "[I feel] just happiness. To set our goal and to accomplish it . . . You hope everyone has that feeling. You have a goal and work hard and you accomplish it. . . . It's a great feeling."

Still a football lover, LeBron shoots a video at a Dallas-Washington game.

On Michael Jordan . . . "I definitely look at MJ as the greatest. Without MJ, there's no me. He gave me hope. He gave me inspiration as a kid. I still watch MJ tapes to this day. I was watching *Come Fly With Me* and *Jordan's Playground* and *His Airness* on vacation this summer. So I'm watching him all the time, trying to learn from him."

On watching sports analysts on TV during the playoffs . . . "Nope, nope, not really. I don't watch any of it too much during playoffs. Everything's magnified during the playoffs, and I like to get away from it, as far as that aspect of the game—*SportsCenter*, radio talk shows, NBA TV, all that. At that point, I turn my phones off. No communication. I like to kind of just watch movies, watch TV shows, read books."

On his favorite vegetable . . . "Steamed broccoli—I enjoy eating it and it's healthy."

On how he handled losing when he was a kid . . . "It was tough because I thought winning was everything when I was a kid, and my competitive nature would just take over. But I've learned that while it's great to win, you also learn a lot when you lose, and it helps you in the long run."

On a sport he's not too good at playing . . . "I'm terrible at tennis. The ball comes too fast!"

On advice he would give a young athlete . . . "First of all, make sure you're doing it for yourself, you know? You worked hard to get there. Don't let anybody else make your decisions. You should make them and do what's best for your family."

On a promotional visit to China, LeBron goes one-on-one with a young player.

On handling pressure . . . "Just by being myself on and off the court. I don't change just because people expect me to do things. I'm a relaxed person. I love laughing, I love hanging out with my friends. That's the kind of stuff that keeps the stress away. Just being myself."

On reading in front of fans . . . "I went into the playoffs [2012] and wanted to do something different, so I called a friend of mine, and I asked him to give me some books. And I started reading and started bringing them to the game. I wasn't doing it for attention. I was actually reading

LeBron says reading is very important. Here he reads to a group of kids at an Akron library.

High-flying LeBron slam dunks another two-pointer during the 2013 playoffs!

the books. But the reception I got from so many people . . . just teachers and parents saying that their kid has been coming up to them saying they wanted to read this book I was reading, or they wanted to read a book that was in that genre because I was reading it . . . it was powerful."

On what basketball means to him . . . "The game of basketball means everything to me. This is love. Definitely love. I had to practice and I had to make sacrifices, but basketball has given me so many opportunities."

LEBRON'S UP CLOSE AND PERSONAL FACTS!

CHECK OUT OUR MINI LEBRON JAMES SCRAPBOOK!

NBA LEGEND JULIUS "DR. J" ERVING CONGRATULATES LEBRON ON HIS ROOKIE OF THE YEAR AWARD.

FIRSTS

FIRST IN 2003 DRAFT
LeBron was chosen first in the 2003 NBA draft.

YOUNGEST ROOKIE OF THE YEAR
LeBron was the youngest NBA player ever to be named Rookie of the Year.

FIRST WATCH
LeBron's first watch was a Swatch given to him by his mother.

FIRST NBA MVP FOR LeBRON AND THE CAVS
In 2009, LeBron won his first NBA MVP. He received the award at a ceremony in the gym of St. Vincent-St. Mary High School. The MVP award was also a first for any player in Cavs history!

funfact: LeBron was **scouted** by pro teams when he was only in ninth grade!

LIKE FATHER, LIKE SON

LeBron's older son, LeBron James Jr. ("Bronny"), is jump-shooting right into the family sport! Proud dad, LeBron, sent out an Instagram of Bronny at a school basketball game. "Bronny went for 25-8-8 tonight. He getting better and better. Couple euro steps looking like @dwyanewade and what I like most is his unselfishness #HeGotNext #StriveForGreatness." The nine-year-old looked like a chip off the old block!

LeBron Gets Starstruck:

"The first time I met Michael Jordan, I was a sophomore in high school, and it was an unbelievable experience for me. It didn't even feel like he was on the face of the Earth. This guy was more like an angel, like an alien or something."

LEBRON & FIRST LADY MICHELLE OBAMA

The Miami Heat made a visit to the White House so President Obama could congratulate them on their 2013 NBA championship victory. Some of the team's players also made a "Let's Move" public service announcement with Michelle Obama. While Dwyane Wade, Chris Bosh, and Ray Allen were being interviewed for the video, LeBron and Michelle were behind them LOL-ing it up. They munched on apples when the guys talked about energy food, drank water when the topic was keeping hydrated, and then LeBron held up a mini-hoop while Michelle slam-dunked a ball!

LEBRON'S NIKE SUNSHINE

In October 2013, LeBron starred in a Nike commercial for his new LeBron 11 Sneakers. The hoops hero wanted to spotlight his kicks and the Heat's hometown, Miami. Called Training Day, the commercial features kids joining LeBron as he bicycles and jogs through the city, waves to men playing dominoes, swims in the ocean, and plays an outdoor pickup game of b-ball. About his day, LeBron said, "So much fun, man. The message is obvious. I want people to feel like they're one with me and I had a lot of fun, shooting all over Miami and to have all those kids, it was good."

LeBron's Biggest Fear:
"I'm afraid of failure. I want to succeed so bad that I become afraid of failing. . . . [How to overcome it?] Just win. Keep winning and I don't have to worry about it. Keep winning."

CAN YOU KEEP A SECRET?

LeBron had a major growth spurt the summer before his sophomore year in high school. He grew six inches to a height of 6'6" (he later grew two more inches and topped out at 6'8"). But back then, LeBron didn't want to be measured anymore! Why? "I don't want anybody to know my identity. I'm like a superhero. Call me: 'Basketball Man.'" Tough secret to keep when you tower over everyone and you're the best!

FRIENDS FOREVER

Jay-Z:
"I love him. He do what he do. He takes care of his business, he works hard and everything is love. He got God-given talent."

Derek Jeter:
"The first thing that strikes you is his sheer size and athleticism. . . . He's down to earth. Most people in LeBron's position aren't as grounded. . . . He's given back so much to Ohio and Akron, his hometown."

Dwyane Wade:
"He's off the planet. He's not even the best player on the planet. He's somewhere else right now—the galaxy."

SWEET TWEET Q&A

On January 12, 2014, LeBron held a 5 a.m., 15-minute Twitter-thon where fans could ask him questions. Here's a sample:

Q: "@KingJames favorite rapper besides Jay-Z[?]"
A: "@Drake"

Q: "@KingJames what's your favorite ever moment in basketball?"
A: "Winning a Championship"

Q: "@KingJames Do you ever feel nervous before a game?"
A: "All the time"

Q: "@KingJames do you think that Kobe Bryant is good?"
A: "What! Did u think Jaws was a huge shark? Exactly"

Q: "@KingJames What's your favorite shot to take?"
A: "A lay-up. Lol"

Q: "@KingJames what motivates [you] to strive for greatness?"
A: "My family and the kids that I inspire throughout the world"

Q: @KingJames what's your definition of success[?]"
A: "Happiness"

LeBron knows where
the b-ball goes—right
in the hoop. Swish!

UP THE COURT WITH LEBRON

ON HIS WAY TO THE NBA HALL OF FAME!

So what does the future hold for LeBron James? You don't need a crystal ball to predict that he's going to be driving toward the hoop for a long, long time. His hard work, dedication, and sheer determination have made him a better player year after year. He's also learned more about the emotional and mental aspects of the game. He's learned that basketball is a team sport, no matter whether he is playing in a pickup game or a championship matchup. In high school, he had Little Dru, Sian, Willie, and Romeo. They worked like a fine-tuned clock. On the Miami Heat, he has Chris Bosh and Dwyane Wade, the NBA's own mini dream team. That chemistry works . . . but professional athletes don't stand still. Things always change, whether it's due to injury, age, or a move to another team.

LeBron has to deal with all of these possibilities every day, and in the summer of 2014, he chose to declare himself a free agent. That means he could sign a new contract with the Heat or move to another team.

No matter what he decides, LeBron will still be working on his lifelong quest: to be the best. When a reporter from ESPN asked him what he would have to do to become the greatest of all time, LeBron thought for a moment and then said, "My goal is to be the best of all time, and that means maximizing everything I have. And I feel if I can maximize my game, then I can be ranked as if not the greatest, then one of the greatest. Obviously, I have to keep winning. . . . And I feel I will continue to win as long as I can stay healthy and be a part of something special."

With that attitude, you can rest assured that no matter what direction LeBron chooses, he will always be special!

Fame Trap

"It can [mess you up] if you're not built for it, if you're not ready to take on that challenge. I was ready because I had my friends. They were my shelter; they made me stay humble."

Resources

BOOKS

Gregory, Josh. *LeBron James*. New York: Bearport Publishing, 2014.
James, LeBron, and Buzz Bissinger. *Shooting Stars*. New York: Penguin Press, 2009.
Savage, Jeff. *LeBron James*. Minneapolis: Lerner Publications Company, 2014.

ARTICLES

ESPN The Magazine, **October 28, 2013 issue**
"LeBron James Confidential"

Sports Illustrated, **April 30, 2012 issue**
"After Tumultuous First Year in Miami, LeBron Returns a New Man"

Facts for Now

Visit this Scholastic Web site for more information on **LeBron James**: www.factsfornow.scholastic.com Enter the keywords **LeBron James**

Glossary

centers *(SEN-turz)* especially tall players on a basketball team who usually position themselves near the basket, where they can use their height as an advantage

playoffs *(PLAY-awfs)* the final games at the end of a sports season that determine which teams will face off for the championship

protégé *(PROH-tuh-zhay)* someone chosen by an experienced or knowledgeable mentor to receive advice, training, or other guidance

running back *(RUH-ning BAK)* an offensive football position; running backs receive handoffs from a quarterback and attempt to move the ball by running past the opposing team's defenders

scouted *(SKOUT-id)* observed by representatives from colleges or professional teams

starter *(STAR-tur)* a player who is chosen to be in a team's lineup at the very beginning of a game or match; usually a team's best players

Index

Allen, Ray, 39
All-Star Game, 19, 20

birth, 6, 13, 20
books, 32, 34–35
Bosh, Chris, 13, 24, 25, 30, 39, 45
Boston Celtics, 20, 21
Bryant, Kobe, 43

Caito, Joe, 9
championships, 8, 14, 16, 17, 18, 20, 22, 25, 26, 27, 28, 29, 29, 31, 39, 43
Charlotte Hornets, 25
childhood, 6, 8–12, 33
China, 23, 28, 33
Cleveland Cavaliers basketball team, 18, 19, 20, 21, 22, 23, 25–26, 37
Cleveland *Plain Dealer* newspaper, 23
Cotton, Lee, 12
Cotton, Sian, 11–12, 14, 16, 17, 44–45

Dallas Mavericks, 24, 26
Decision, The (television show), 22, 24
Detroit Pistons, 19
draft, 22, 37

East Dragons football team, 8–9, 10
education, 8, 9, 11, 12, 17
Erving, Julius "Dr. J," 36
ESPN, 24, 45

Fact Files, 12–13, 14–15
foods, 15, 33, 39
football, 8–9, 10, 13, 14, 15, 32
free agency, 21

goals, 11, 18, 21, 31, 45

height, 13, 41

James, Bryce Maximus (son), 13
James, Gloria (mother), 6, 8, 9, 10, 11, 13, 24, 37
James, LeBron, Jr. (son), 13, 21–22, 38
James, Savannah (wife), 13, 42
Jay Z, 15, 42
jersey numbers, 13, 21
Jeter, Derek, 42, 42
Jordan, Michael, 13, 13, 32, 38
Joyce, Dru, 11, 16
Joyce, Dru, III, 11, 12, 14, 16, 17, 17, 44–45

Kelker, Bruce, 8–9

McGee, Willie, 14, 16, 17, 44–45
McClelland, Anthony (father), 6, 13
Miami Heat basketball team, 22, 23, 24, 25, 26, 27, 28, 29, 30, 31, 35, 39, 40, 44, 45
"Mr. Basketball" awards, 13, 21
MVP awards, 20, 24, 28, 29, 37

nicknames, 7, 10, 13

Obama, Barack, 25, 27, 39
Obama, Michelle, 39
Oklahoma City Thunder, 24, 28
Olajuwon, Hakeem, 26–27, 28

Olympic Games, 23, 25, 28
Orlando Magic, 20

playoffs, 19, 20, 21, 23, 24, 28, 32
PSAs (public service announcements), 29, 39
public opinion, 23–25, 25–26

records, 19–20, 21, 29
Rookie of the Year award, 23, 36, 37

Sacramento Kings, 19
San Antonio Spurs, 19, 23, 25, 29
Shooting Stars basketball team, 11–12
Shooting Stars (LeBron James), 16, 17
social media, 13, 43
Spoelstra, Erik, 28
Sports Illustrated magazine, 21
St. Vincent-St Mary High School, *7, 8, 10,* 13, 14, 16–17, 20–*21,* 22, 37, 41
Summit Lake Hornets basketball team, 11, 12, 14

Training Day commercial, 40
Travis, Romeo, 16, 17, 44–45
Twitter, 13, 43

USA Today newspaper, 23–24

Wade, Dwyane, 13, 24, 25, 29, 30, 38, 39, 42, 45
Walker, Frank, Jr., 10
Walker, Frank, Sr., 9, 10, 11
wedding, 42

Acknowledgments

Page 5: *Hard Work:* ESPN The Magazine, October 28, 2013
Page 9: *School Days:* Sports Illustrated Kids
Page 11: *Speedy Learner:* Sports Illustrated Kids
Page 12: *Basketball Boy:* Seventeen, February 2004
Page 14: *Basketball Alternative*: Nickelodeon magazine
Page 15: *SpongeBob SquarePants:* ABC-TV News, February 18, 2013; *Jay-Z:* Seventeen, February 2004
Page 16: *Junior year:* Shooting Stars
Page 17: *Last high school game:* Shooting Stars

Page 18: *Being a Champ:* Sports Illustrated, April 30, 2012
Page 21: *Achieving Your Goals:* Grantland.com;
Page 22: *Miami move reaction:* USA Today, December 6, 2011
Page 24: *The Move:* People.com
Page 26: *Working with Hakeem Olajuwon:* Grantland.com
Page 27: *White House Visit:* Blackenterprise .com;
Page 28: *Coach Spoelstra:* Grantland.com
Page 31: *NBA championship:* hoopshype.com

Page 32: *Michael Jordan:* ESPN.go.com; *Sports Analysts:* ESPN.go.com
Page 33: *Favorite Vegetable:* Nickelodeon magazine; *Losing:* Nickelodeon magazine; *Tennis:* Seventeen, February 2004; *Advice:* Seventeen, February 2004;
Page 34: *Pressure:* Sports Illustrated Kids; *Reading:* ESPN The Magazine, December 10, 2012
Page 35: *Basketball:* The-talks.com
Page 38: *LeBron Gets Starstruck:* Maxim, November 2009; *Like Father, Like*

Son: sports.yahoo.com
Page 40: *LeBron's Nike Sunshine:* Huffington Post, October 28, 2013
Page 41: *LeBron's Biggest Fear:* ESPN.go.com; *Can You Keep a Secret?:* complex.com;
Page 42: *Jay-Z:* MTV.com; *Derek Jeter:* Time, April 29–May 6, 2013; *Dwyane Wade:* USA Today, February 9, 2013
Page 43: *Sweet Tweet Q&A:* news.rapgenius .com
Page 45: *Fame Trap:* The-talks.com

About the Author

Marie Morreale is the author of many official and unofficial celebrity biographies. She attended New York University as an English/creative writing major and began her writing and editorial career in New York City. As the editor of teen/music magazines *Teen Machine* and *Jam!*, she covered TV, film, and music personalities and interviewed superstars such as Michael Jackson, Britney Spears, and Justin Timberlake/*NSYNC. Morreale was also an editor/writer at Little Golden Books.

Today, she is the executive editor, Media, of Scholastic Classroom Magazines and supplies the editors with content on pop-culture, sports, news, and special events. Morreale lives in New York City and is entertained daily by her two Maine coon cats, Cher and Sullivan.